MEDITATIONS FOR HEALTH

MEDITATIONS FOR

HEALTH

BY NANCY BURKE

WINGS BOOKS ■ NEW YORK ■ NEW JERSEY

All rights reserved.
This 1995 edition is published by Wings Books,
distributed by Random House Value Publishing, Inc.,
40 Engelhard Avenue, Avenel, New Jersey 07001.

Random House
New York • Toronto • London • Sydney • Auckland

Jacket art: The Masked Ball, Rene Magritte
Design: Nora Sheehan
Production supervision by Roméo Enriquez

Printed and bound in Mexico

Library of Congress Cataloging-in-Publication Data

Burke, Nancy
Meditations for health / by Nancy Burke.
p.   cm.
ISBN 0-517-12415-7 (hardcover)
1. Health—Miscellanea.   I. Title.
RA776.5.B87   1995   95-15201
613—dc20   CIP

8   7   6   5   4   3   2   1

FOR THE CHILDREN

Daniel, David, Megan . . . Jennifer, William . . . Katja . . . and my own, my one and only . . . Kaitlin,
because they endure

ACKNOWLEDGEMENTS

For their love and kindness, strength and support, humor and compassion, across time
and distance, I am forever grateful to my mother and stepfather, Nancy and George
Smith; to my sister, brothers, and their spouses: Kelly and Richard Stuart, Jeffrey and
Anje Burke, and William and Janice Burke; to my friends: Christopher and Marian
Toy, Donna Caldwell and Jim McDonald, Robert and Kris Mallett, Joanne Dwyer, and
Jill Prior Fuller; and to Kate Sheehan Hartson, who, with this book, gave me an un-
merited gift: a little piece of immortality.

ABOUT THE AUTHOR

Nancy Burke is a writer, book and magazine editor, and a cancer and heart attack sur-
vivor. She lives with her daughter in New England.

In the name of God, stop a moment, cease your work, look around you.

LEO TOLSTOY

Many books on health and healing are filled with sad stories of men and women who question how they have been living only after their lives have been threatened by illness. Then they frantically search for time with lovers, children, friends. They long to take up again the avocations and good intentions laid aside in deference to career. Too late they realize that they have brought to their *jobs* all the passion and commitment that they might have brought to their life. ▪ Our work is not our life. We will rarely be measured by what we do for a living. Rather, we will be remembered for who we were in the company of other men and women and how we touched others in the fullness of our hearts. ▪ It is not healthy for body or soul to reserve our real living for occasional weekends or two weeks in July. Most of us must work. But we can work with less fervor and live with more passion.

LUNCHEON ON THE GRASS, CLAUDE MONET

If there is any posture that disturbs a suffering man or woman, it is aloofness.

HENRI J. M. NOUWEN

Health researchers claim that one in four people will face a serious illness in their lifetime. This means there is a small chance we will become ill, but a big chance someone we care about will. Can we be there for him or her? Every person who has battled disease or disability has an apocryphal tale about a friend or family member who couldn't come through for him. ■ We may distance ourselves emotionally from a suffering man or woman because we are frightened. Disease and disability, particularly when they are sudden or accidental, underscore the capriciousness of fate, the folly of believing we are anything but mortal. If it happened to him or her, it *can* happen to you or me. Or our fear may masquerade as anger. Someone who is very ill cannot fully be there for us anymore, may even leave us for good. Who among us wants to be left behind? ■ We can talk through our fear and look at our anger when someone we love is ill. Fear is understandable and anger is forgivable.

A BLUE-CLAD WOMAN, PAUL GAUGUIN

There is a strength in knowing that it can be borne
Although it tear.

EMILY DICKINSON

How wonderful that God makes us such inherently courageous beings. We love again, we raise children, we look for another job. Sometimes we even stare down disease, brandishing our humanity, even as our bodies fail us. And if our spirits fail us too, as they must from time to time, the world is full of brave people and brave tales from which we can grab a handful of courage.

When I was very ill, I had to receive weekly intravenous treatments. This went on for almost two years. Somewhere in the middle I lost my courage. It is hard to say which collapsed first, my soul or my veins, but collapse they both did. One day the search for a healthy vein became too painful. I pushed the needle away and cried. A nurse brought to my side a young girl, of about ten, who had battled cancer all her life. This child smiled at me and said, "You should have got one of these." Lifting her T-shirt, she showed me the hole that had been cut into her abdomen so that she could receive her treatments through a permanent plastic port. Then she put her hand, so small and soft, on mine and said, "You can take it." And I did.

PORTRAIT OF MLLE. IRÈNE CAHEN D'ANVERS,
PIERRE-AUGUSTE RENOIR

Some of us wear our good health like a medieval hair shirt. Life becomes an exercise in *I don't* and *I cannot* and *I must*. This is not healthful living, it is doing penance. And it is a posture that offends more than it inspires. ■ I once worked with a woman who passionately pursued a lower cholesterol count. Every lunchtime, she noisily ate just one apple and tsk-tsked over the fat content of her co-workers' lunches. At the end of six months this woman had lost some weight, lowered her cholesterol count a bit, and secured the enmity of every employee in the firm. ■ We know what we have to do to stay healthy or to get healthy. We eat and drink good things, just enough to keep us going. We move and breathe and get our hearts beating a bit faster. We exercise our sense of humor. We sleep when we are tired. We relax and have fun every chance we get. We do all this because we love ourselves and we love life. We never forget to wear our good health, but we wear it casually.

WOMAN POURING, PORTUGUESE STILL LIFE,
ROBERT DELAUNAY

P

I am not a phoenix yet, but here among the ashes,
it may be that the pain is chiefly that of new wings trying to push through.

MAY SARTON

erhaps we are done an injustice by some New Age writers, who imply that serious illness is always a revelatory experience from which we will emerge transcendent. That's a gamble no one should have to parlay. Viewing the world through a lens shaded by pain and infirmity may result in a vision colored more by fear and anger, less by peace and acceptance. ■ It is an extraordinary person who can sift through the detritus of her pain and find illumination there. Equally extraordinary is our expectation that sick people should do that. We often ask this of them because *we* are made more comfortable when a sick person frames his pain with spiritual or literary platitudes, or is quietly resigned to her fate. Even doctors and nurses quickly flee the patient who rages too loudly against the night. There is rarely anything redemptory about failing health. I have never met a sick person who wouldn't exchange his bad health for good health.

BOUQUET OF FLOWERS, TULIPS AND LILIES,
MOISE KISLING

T

here is a young girl I see almost every day running along our backcountry road. When the wind whips her baggy sweatsuit close to her body I see that she is nothing but bone. Her face, too, is classically anorexic: all dangerous cheekbones and large eyes sunk into dark sockets. I've watched her run for nine months now, seeing her grow thinner and more fragile every day. She is not like the other runners I see on my walks, who wave as they fly past. They are all rounded muscle, strong, sweaty, solid. My girl is grim and solitary, an insubstantial slash on the landscape. I wonder who her family is and why they allow this self-punishment. But I know they cannot stop her any more than I. She started running (and stopped eating) because she heard some wicked voice inside telling her she wasn't right, she wasn't *thin* enough. ■ If you run or walk or workout because you're afraid of having a coronary, of aging, of getting fat— that's *okay*. Anything to get you off the couch! As long as you understand you may get ill despite all your best efforts. You will grow old if you're lucky, and it can be fabulous. And being thin is no guarantee against misery.

NUDE WITH ORANGES, HENRI MATISSE

The body is a universe in itself and must be held as sacred as anything in creation. . . .
It is dangerous to forget the body as sacramental.

MAY SARTON

Like many others who have found themselves in trouble, I returned to the church of my childhood when things seemed their darkest: Illness, and the threat of death, had brought me to my knees, and I was not prepared. It took me a few years to find a body of believers and a pastor with whom I could sit once a week without feeling I must jump up, screaming, and run for cover. My church is in much trouble: Arrogant fundamentalists grow larger in number and violent in speech; they seem to delight in pushing us gentler folk against the wall. ■ Still I go. I am always reminded that I am not alone, and that is healthy. And I am always led to find something about which to be grateful, and that is healing. ■ At our Thanksgiving Mass this year, a day we hold as sacred as any other holy day, there was a moment in the liturgy when we stood, held hands, and said the Lord's Prayer together. I held the hand of my eight-year-old, who held the hand of an eighty-year-old, and the circle moved on, hand over hand, unbroken, among the five hundred in church. The presence of God was indisputable, the power of faith breathtaking. In our collective gratitude, we all became, at that moment, immortal.

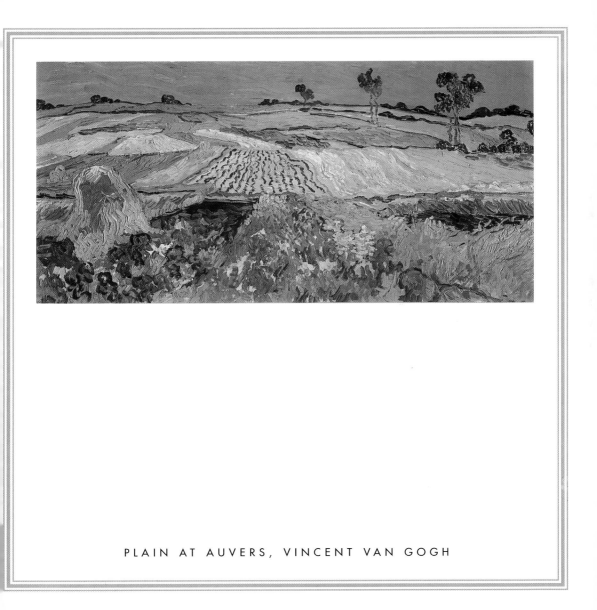

PLAIN AT AUVERS, VINCENT VAN GOGH

One of my problems is that I internalize everything.
I can't express anger; I grow a tumor instead.

WOODY ALLEN

Anger was very fashionable in the seventies (before we learned that an episode of bad temper could land us in a coronary care unit). Encounter groups sprang up across the country, and otherwise normal people spent hours screaming at and punching pillows. This was called "venting one's rage." Fortunately encounter groups soon went the way of disco. ▪ Letting go of unhealthy behavior is difficult work. Getting a handle on anger, with its delicious rush of self-righteousness, is particularly hard. Many of us cling to a kind of quiet fury, waving incidents with family or friends, church or jobs, that we believe justify our rage. Anger becomes as necessary to our being as breathing. But anger so rarely accomplishes anything good. And at its worst, it batters the heart, sullies the soul, and is altogther enervating. When you're not feeling well to begin with, that's an awful place to be. ▪ I don't know how much anger contributed to my own bad health, but it surely hurt my recovery. I needed all the strength and courage only heart and soul can provide. Anger was stealing my future. Practicing not getting angry, a day at a time, has been a tough job. I have found only two antidotes to anger: forgiveness and walking away.

WHITE ZIG ZAG, WASSILY KANDINSKY

Never assume you possess everything you will need to weather rough waters. You probably don't. Be cautious about overestimating your strengths. Paradoxically, what serves us well when life is on an even keel (toughness, self-reliance, putting all our faith in one person or one thing) may be precisely the thing that hinders recovery. Likewise don't underestimate your weaknesses. Our less obvious flaws (fear, mistrust, lack of confidence) may rise to the surface in bad times and become our complete undoing. ■ Everything you will need, or long for, when rough weather hits is exactly everything you should be cultivating *now*, to make your good life even better: a belief in something greater than yourself; respect for body, mind, and spirit; a rich interior life, framed with prayer, contemplation, or meditation; a supportive family; loving friends; the ability to forgive and the desire to serve; a personal code of right and wrong and behavior that reflects it; a reverence for beauty, honor, and grace.

ON THE THAMES, ANDRE DERAIN

T

o get healthy, we often must wrestle (again and again) one very insidious personal demon. For some it is too much weight. For others, too much drink. Still others do battle with depression or anxiety. For me it was smoking. Even after I became ill, I struggled for a long time to put down cigarettes for good. And such is the complexity of addiction and denial that I could find justification for nicotine abuse in my very illness: On the one hand, I had one of the few cancers that hadn't yet been linked to smoking; on the other, I was under so much stress from being ill, how could I stop? This is embarrassing to relate, in retrospect, but anyone who has been (or is) thoroughly addicted to anything will recognize the hoops we addicts jump through to continue using. Then I developed heart problems in the middle of treatment. And the dance was over.

■ Smoking may kill you, or put you in the hospital. And if you wind up in the hospital, you may *wish* you were dead. You can't smoke in hospitals anymore. They have smoke alarms in all the bathrooms and stairwells. And if you try to sneak out a back exit with your IV bottle tucked under your arm and your hospital gown tucked between your legs, a security guard *will* find you and bring you back to your room and tell your doctor. And you will look and feel as foolish as I did.

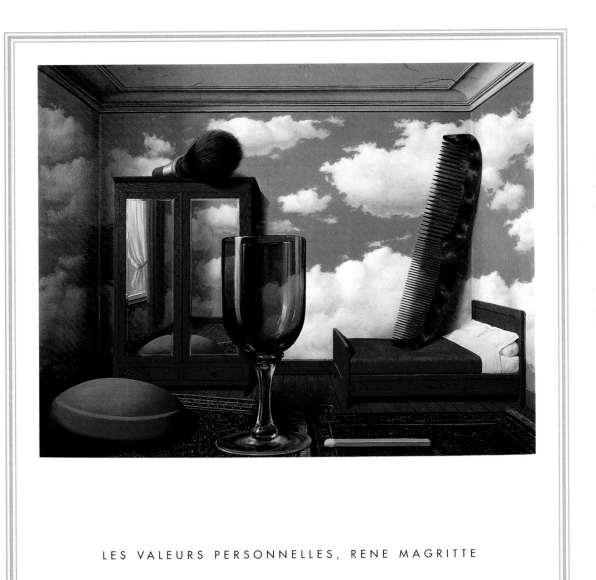

LES VALEURS PERSONNELLES, RENE MAGRITTE

The cure for anything is salt water—sweat, tears, or the sea.

ISAK DINESEN

Medical science has given us some extraordinary gifts. Antibiotics and vaccines save millions of us daily from bacteria and viruses that were lethal just a century ago. Others of us live better and longer because a pill we take regulates our heart rate or blood pressure, our sugar or hormone level. Painkillers make many a recovery easier and faster and many a death more peaceful. This is medicine at its most powerful, and we should be grateful for it. ■ Still we must be cautious about looking for relief in a bottle. We were meant, first and always, to care for ourselves. When we stop believing that relief is always "out there," and look instead to ourselves first, we will see we carry within ourselves much potential for healing. Many of us would not need our heart medications if we took ourselves out each day for a good run or a long walk, if we cared as much about what we put into our bodies as we do about how we dress them up. Not all of us would need our tranquilizers and antidepressants if we were easier on ourselves, if we honored the fact that there is a dark side to each of us and to many of the moments of our lives, and that we sometimes need to cry and other times need to rage. We would not have to arm ourselves, with alcohol and drugs, against the bogeymen of the night, if we took ourselves out more often, into the sunlight.

ON THE BEACH, EDOUARD MANET

S leep is one of the most potent and least expensive ways to get well and stay well. Cultivate the habit of a good night's sleep and you will feel stronger, perform better, and look healthier. One of the reasons many of us are so thoroughly sleep deprived is because we work too hard, too often, and then wind up trying to cram all our real living into a few evening hours. Look around you. Those sallow-skinned, dull-eyed, short-tempered people you live and work with probably don't need vitamins or a psychiatrist or a vacation; they just need some sleep. ■ If you cheat on sleep to grab some fun because you work too much, all three are eventually going to suffer, along with your health. Our bodies need sleep to shake off all the little indignities we do them each day and to recharge for the morrow. When we are recovering from an illness or surgery, our bodies do their greatest healing while we sleep. Likewise our minds need respite from all the furious cogitations we put them through each day. Quiet minds find answers far more quickly than restless ones: Haven't you ever woken from a good night's sleep with the solution to a problem you'd spent days ruminating over? Finally, and perhaps most importantly, our spirits need to dream: to stoke our creative fires, to throw a net over our demons, to reinfuse our souls.

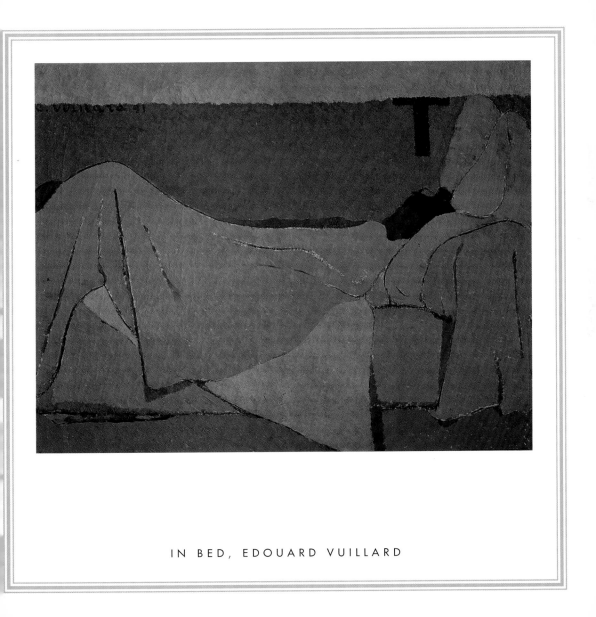

IN BED, EDOUARD VUILLARD

It is part of the cure to wish to be cured.

SENECA

Getting healthy can be glorious, but it's also hard work. If we are older, and have a lifetime of bad habits to put behind us, getting healthy may even involve some pain. The thirty pounds we want to lose look (and *are*) a long way off. When we put down our last drink or cigarette, it may feel as though we will *never* stop thinking about it. And after that first run around the lake or two-mile walk, our body will ache in places we didn't know we had! ■ We are most at risk for giving up on our new, healthier lifestyles at the beginning of the journey, when the going is slow and rough, the benefits far down the road. Before we start any new regimen, we need to hold our good intentions sacred; fix in our minds an image of ourselves the way we want to be—thinner, stronger, faster, free; and then stop being so results oriented. Instead we should prepare ourselves for a long, easy haul. That's where the real fun is anyway. Getting healthy should never be about competing, with ourselves or anyone else. A healthy lifestyle isn't something we win or lose. It's a process. Eventually a way of life. Ultimately something that becomes so natural, we will do it as reflexively as we breathe.

TWO BOATS, ANDRE DERAIN

And if the earthly no longer knows your name, whisper to the silent earth:
I'm flowing. To the flashing water say: I am.
RAINER MARIA RILKE

Despite our best efforts, some of us will never achieve or recover good health. Others will lose the battle with illness entirely and come to know they are dying. We can turn that knowledge into a gift, for ourselves and for those we love. Now we can take the time to savor, like never before, every rise and set of the sun, every phase of every moon, each rain shower and cloudless sky, all the rich and myriad sights and sounds and smells that are the ordinary and extraordinary stuff of these, our last days. Then we can make our good-byes with a full heart, in the arms of those we love, ever mindful that these are *their* last memories, too, and that we want to leave them with the very best. ■ If we all approached each of our days as if they were the last, perhaps we would finally understand that a life well lived is our greatest responsibility and our ultimate glory. The prospect of death wouldn't be so frightening. Of course we are a relentlessly hopeful group—that's what makes us human—and who are we *not* to believe we can live forever? In many ways we do.

CATALONIAN LANDSCAPE, PABLO PICASSO

T

he second time I became ill, about the only good things I had going for me were that I was still alive *and* that I had already spent twelve months battling the hairy beast that's our medical system. I had learned that some doctors are great, others are good, and a few rare ones are miserable. So this time, before I began a course of radiation, I had a conference with the head of radiology in our state's largest hospital. After discussing my treatment plan, the doctor asked me what my expectations about treatment were. I thought about my four-year-old daughter and said, "I'd like to see my daughter graduate from high school." To which she replied, "That will never happen." Now, most of us know we are mortal, but few of us have our mortality so roughly served up. (Later, the nurse told me that the doctor hadn't wanted me to have any "false hopes.") ■ I found another radiologist. When we had our conference, she asked me if I was planning to get pregnant and, if so, to take precautions because radiation might damage the child. She made no promises. But what a life-affirming statement! ■ Don't let anyone ever rob you of your hopes—the big ones or the little ones. And whether you're well or struggling with an illness, for God's sake, surround yourself with winners.

DR. GEORGES VIAU IN HIS DENTAL OFFICE
ATTENDING ANNETTE ROUSSEL,
EDOUARD VUILLARD

You can't pray a lie.

MARK TWAIN

Many of us turn to God when we are troubled, and prayer is our only vehicle. But sometimes, when we are fearful or in pain, when we need to pray the most, it is almost impossible to find our voice. This is when the prayers of others can be so special. When people pray "for" us, they are doing the praying we cannot do for ourselves. And others' prayers are no less powerful than our own to heal and comfort. ■ When we can pray for ourselves, we may bring to the altar a desperate heart, a voice filled with more questions than acceptance: How can I pray for relief when so many others get none? Do I deserve extra time with my child or spouse? Am I wrong to wish this over? Is there a purpose to this pain? These broken, hesitant prayers echo no less loudly than self-assured ones. ■ Even when we fall to our knees in anger, wondering if our prayers are heard at all, and by whom, and why they are never answered, our angry voices sound no less sweet than those filled with love. ■ When every prayer is an act of faith, it can never ring hollow: You will never pray a lie.

SUNFLOWERS, CLAUDE MONET

He lived at a little distance from his body,
regarding his own acts with doubtful side-glances.

JAMES JOYCE

Do you? ■ Athletes, runners, and others who work their bodies don't. They can look in a mirror without wincing, run up two flights of stairs without getting winded, and help a neighbor move a couch without strapping on a truss. They can also sit at meditation or prayer longer and more comfortably, focusing on the pleasure of contemplation rather than the pain in their neck and knees. Even when their bodies aren't perfect, and few are, they can take pride in the fact that they have gotten a mighty return for very little investment— thirty minutes a day, every other day. ■ Respecting our bodies through exercise, be it gentle or vigorous, and honoring these extraordinary machines for their capabilities and their limitations, is the beginning of good health. For once we begin to honor the body as a whole, we are inevitably led to honor its parts. It's the height of foolery to take our hearts out for a good run in the morning and spend our lunch hour wolfing down a cheeseburger and fries. And we are engaged in an awful denial when we spend Friday afternoons at a health club doing the Nautilus circuit and Friday evenings at a tavern throwing back half a case of beer.

THE TEAM FROM CARDIFF, ROBERT DELAUNAY

Nothing is more desirable than to be released from an affliction,
but nothing is more frightening than to be divested of a crutch.

JAMES BALDWIN

Some advocates of mind-body medicine encourage patients to blame themselves for their disease. As part of their treatment, they are asked to consider all the wonderful benefits they get from being seriously ill that they couldn't get when they were healthy: excitement . . . drama . . . attention . . . love! When the patient finally learns to give himself all these terrific things in a healthier way, then he may be cured. Or at least die a better human being. Proponents of this theory have obviously never spent two days wrapped around a toilet bowl shaking off the effects of chemotherapy. Nor have they spent any time in a children's cancer ward or AIDS unit. I have little patience for facile New Age healers who are so eager to rearrange the psyches of vulnerable people. And then write books about it. ■ There's a marked difference between luxuriating in self-blame and taking responsibility for changing things that may have contributed to illness or that might hurt recovery. A wise and compassionate healer gently shows her patients the difference.

STILL-LIFE WITH POMEGRANATES, HENRI MATISSE

My advice is don't spend your money on therapy. Spend it in a record store.

WIM WENDERS

Someday I may get to personally thank Patti La Belle for sharing her magnificent voice and extraordinary heart in song. Until then, this will have to do. ■ Every week, for two winters and two summers, as I drove to and from the cancer clinic for treatments, I played her renditions of "Somewhere Over the Rainbow" and "There's a Winner in You" over and over. When I was frightened and thought I couldn't make one more trip, I played those songs to get me there. Afterward, when I was tired and afraid I couldn't make the drive home, I played them again. My spirits never failed to recover, and the miles just flew by. I found such courage and hope in her passionate music. In the midst of the darkest time of my life, that voice made me feel grateful to be alive. ■ Pavarotti singing *"Nessun Dorma"* will do this too. Most anything by Puccini. Or Pat Metheny's "If I Could." Aaron Neville singing "The Lord's Prayer." Or Barber's "Adagio for Strings." This is music touched by God. ■ There's a song for everyone, one incalculable mix of melody and magic that so neatly wraps the heart that we are lifted out of the here and now. And something in us is healed. Search for your song.

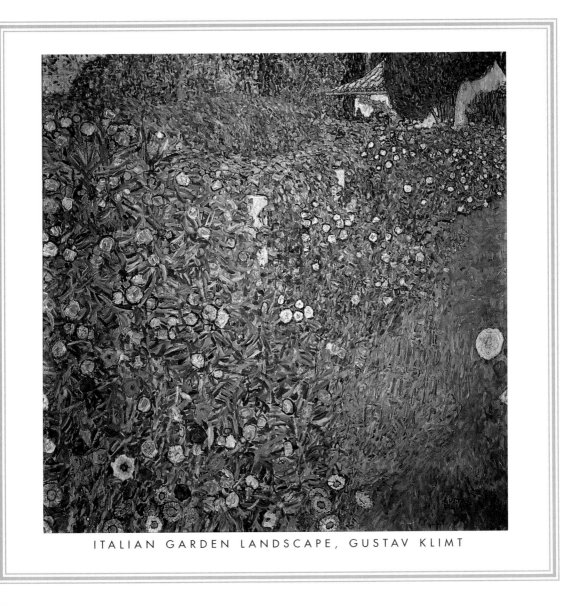

ITALIAN GARDEN LANDSCAPE, GUSTAV KLIMT

W

Sitting quietly, doing nothing,
Spring comes and the grass grows by itself.

ZENRIN

e know now that meditation isn't only for the spiritually adept. It can do wonderful things for the body. Cardiologists recommend it to their patients to reduce stress. It can also help in managing pain and speeding up recovery from surgery. But meditation may be most powerful for what it offers a wounded heart. Try meditating for ten minutes a day. Just for you. No teacher, no expectations. Just you, in a quiet, darkened room, sitting or lying down. Don't worry about posture (or candles and incense and mantras). That's not for now. You are not looking for enlightenment, for answers, for a mystical experience. (Though all that may be there in time.) Now it's just you and your breathing. Looking for some respite, to step out of the world for a moment or two. Gently and slowly breathe through your nose. Then softly let your breath out. Breathe in. Gently. Breathe out. Softly. Just breathe. When we come into this world, the first thing we do is breathe in. Divine inspiration. When we leave this world, the last thing we do is breathe out. Everything in between is just gravy. It's all been taken care of. We leave home and we go home. Children of God. And if we really believe He holds us in the palm of His hand for the journey, then anything can be endured.

HARMONIE ROSE, CLAUDE MONET

Every move is a prayer.

MAN OF THE CROW DOG FAMILY

Long before aerobics became a national pastime and jogging went corporate, most of the world understood that exercise of body was inseparable from exercise of soul. Millions of people in India practice hatha yoga postures—*asanas*—not merely for the physical benefits but because each *asana* uniquely stretches the muscles and strengthens the breath in a way that centers heart, mind, *and* body for meditation. Likewise the gentle movements of Tai Chi are themselves meant to be meditation in motion. They are practiced every morning, by hundreds of people at a time, in public parks throughout Asian countries. In the East physical health and spiritual well-being have always been linked. ■ In the West we are finally beginning to understand that what we eat and how we move (and often, how and if we pray) mightily affect how we think and feel, and therefore who we are. We are at our healthiest when we exercise our bodies, treat them with care, because we know they carry something of the sacred within, a little bit of the Divine.

BLUE DANCERS, EDGAR DEGAS

Between living and dreaming there is a third thing.

Guess it.

ANTONIO MACHADO
Translated by Robert Bly © 1983

It might be living *well*, one day at a time. And though a life measured by days well lived is a relative thing, for many of us it includes a day we've been good to our bodies and prayed for our souls and remembered to be grateful; a day we haven't gotten angry and have tried to be forgiving; a day we've trusted more or doubted less, given much and taken little. ▪ Such an attitude doesn't come easily or naturally. Learning to live well, a day at a time, is slow and careful work. It's important we strike a balance between caring about the people and the world around us—without becoming exhausted—and caring for body and soul—without becoming self-absorbed. ▪ We can find extraordinary examples of just such good living in our neighbors and friends. Often it is those who are the most encumbered, by bad health or disability or age or family problems, who can always seem to find room in their lives to love and learn, listen and share. And it will always be a puzzlement why the fittest among us, brimming with energy and vitality, surrounded by wealth and comfort, are often the least tolerant and giving, the ones who always want more.

STILL LIFE, MAURICE DE VLAMINCK

To be too conscious is an illness—a real thorough-going illness.

FYODOR DOSTOYEVSKY

We all know people who live too much in their heads. (I was one of them myself.) These are the people who must analyze everything *ad nauseam*, and who, when given an hour or two of free time, will, rather than take a walk or kick a ball around or do something silly, instead spend their time worrying over one problem or another, dissecting this situation or that, analyzing that action over this one, again and again and again, often until they make themselves sick. They are the list makers. They are the people who cannot leave their desks at night until every paper is filed away in color-coded folders. They are the friends who unconsciously rearrange the knickknacks on your coffee table. They are the diners who stack the dishes for the waiter. They are the people who are always trying to get the world to "shape up." These people carry around so much unnecessary noise in their heads that a messy world *out there* becomes just so much more painful competition. These are the people who have forgotten how to have fun. ■ If you have to put "Stop Thinking, Have Fun" on your *To Do* list, do it. But do it.

DANCE AT THE MOULIN DE LA GALETTE,
PIERRE-AUGUSTE RENOIR

A
I can, therefore I am.

SIMONE WEIL

few months ago there was much in the news about a young boy who ran away from home. More precisely he ran away from the chemotherapy that was keeping him alive. One day he said, "No more," refused his next dose, tucked his skateboard under his arm, and took off. He stayed away for a long time, for such a sick kid, and he got as far as Texas. People were dumbfounded that a child would take his life into his own hands like that, but I was cheering him all the way. I understood why he was angry. ▪ We can get used to being ill, to being different. We can even come to terms with dying. But we get so tired of being *reminded* we're not the same anymore. What we wouldn't give to leave behind, if only for a while, the hospital smells, and medicine bottles, the white coats and rubber gloves, the machines and syringes, the worried glances and whispered voices. ▪ When the boy came home, his parents did a terrific thing: They left him alone to work it out for himself. He wanted to play, and they let him. There were wonderful pictures of him zooming back and forth on his skateboard, all his friends in tow. And when he had played enough to remember that yes, indeed, he was a child and he could be a child, then he found the courage to say, "Yes. I'll give it one more try."

STILL-LIFE WITH ONIONS, PAUL CEZANNE

When I was a child, I often went to our neighborhood church and sat in that warm, dark, mysterious-smelling place because it was the only quiet harbor in an often chaotic childhood. I might not have kept my sanity if I hadn't had Saint Ignatius to run to, to shut out the noise and slow down the world for an hour or two. Perhaps it is no coincidence that now, when we keep our churches locked up tight, day and night, and religion becomes more ideologically inaccessible too, we are thirsty for spirituality as never before. We yearn for quiet harbors in our lives. ■ For the sake of our sanity and the salvation of our souls, we must sometimes build our own altars, where we can sit or kneel, stop the world, and listen to our hearts. We can do this in an empty corner of our bedroom or kitchen. Place a table there, a candle, a favorite shell or stone or picture. Then shut the door, light the candle, and find again the healing in sitting still, somewhere safe and quiet.

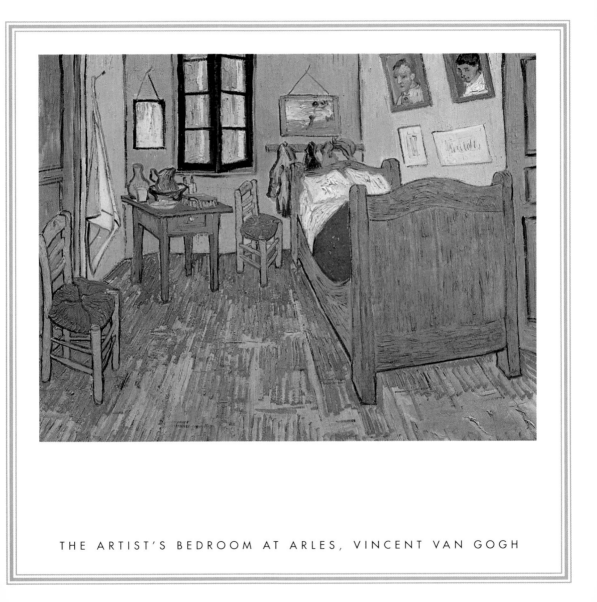

THE ARTIST'S BEDROOM AT ARLES, VINCENT VAN GOGH

T

Be like the bird, who halting in his flight on limb too slight,
yet sings—knowing he has wings.
VICTOR HUGO

he bird doesn't *know* he flies. He has no "faith" in his wings. What he has is a lifetime of little experiences in which, when he feels the edge of the earth disappear and sees nothing but emptiness beneath his feet, still he flies. ▪ If you become very ill, or very troubled, or are simply, like many of us, looking for more meaning in this life, some well-intentioned person will sometime say to you, "Have faith." If faith were such an accessible commodity, something wholly to be "had," like all the other accoutrements of living, we would not still be such a spiritually hungry people, after six-thousand years of every imaginable organized and disorganized theology. Religion cannot give us something we can only ultimately find in the simple weave of our lives. ▪ Perhaps faith emerges, slowly and tentatively, because we humans have a capacity no other animal has: We can look back and reflect. We see, in a lifetime of strung-together experiences—many of which would have felled a lesser soul—that we have endured. We did not endure because we had faith. We find faith because we endure.

WHEATFIELD WITH A LARK, VINCENT VAN GOGH

That I exist is a perpetual surprise which is life.

RABINDRANATH TAGORE

Since I first became ill, I have, with increasing wonder, welcomed in five springs and summers, autumns and winters. I have planted flowers (knowing nothing about gardening) that have thrived in little sun and rocky soil. I have put up (and taken down) five Christmas trees of assorted shapes and sizes, and in between shoveled snow (over and over!). I have swum in oceans and lakes with my child and shook the sand from our towels and sandals at least a hundred times. But I think I like autumn best. I like the slowing down and getting ready for the short, dark haul of winter. I like the hint of eternity in autumn: the fact that we put our summer things away in absolute faith we will use them again. And we do. I never see nature as dying then: I see her gently shutting herself in for a good long night of rest and renewal. And then there is the paradoxical quality of autumn light: Even as the air begins to chill, the sunlight grows brighter and deeper. I love walking in autumn when the leaves have changed but are still on the trees and the road before me is dimpled with splashes of dark and light and all around there is a kind of expectant quiet. I imagine myself caught in a kind of ready-made still life, the stuff that transfixed Monet and Renoir. This is worth living for. This is worth taking care.

LES NYMPHEAS, CLAUDE MONET

Men talk about Bible miracles because there is no miracle in their lives.

Cease to gnaw that crust. There is ripe fruit over your head.

HENRY DAVID THOREAU

Every day brings a miracle, if only for a moment and only if you watch for it. There is no illness so encompassing, no pain so relentless, that we cannot find something to treasure in our day, to remind us of the magic in our lives. ■ Tonight I am taking a scented bath and I have placed some candles along the edge of the tub and put on some soft music in the background. This is going to be my time. I'm going to be healthfully selfish. Then . . . ■ Here comes the cat. Here comes the *other* cat. And here comes the dog. Then along comes the child. She has decided this is a good time to share with me the latest adventures of the *The Boxcar Children*. So she sits on the toilet seat and reads, with great passion, to all of us. ■ Click. In a flash I see how far we have both come and how rich our lives are, though from the outside it may appear we don't have much. Not so. I forgot for a moment that none of this was supposed to happen, that my world was not meant to be filled with so much living, that I got my life back today, again. While my daughter has managed the miracle of pulling together the jumble of letters that became the sounds that became the words that became the book that she reads in the candlelight, I have managed to stick around.

MOTHER AND CHILD, MARY CASSATT

Eternity is a terrible thought. I mean, where's it going to end?

TOM STOPPARD

Sometimes the thought of how very ill I once was makes me think again about death. I drag myself over to the edge of the proverbial abyss and take a peek. Frankly I can't see much there. It's not that I don't believe in a heaven, some great afterlife. I simply can't begin to imagine what it's all about. This world here is much more inviting. Warts and all, living is what I know and like, and living well is what I pray for. It's *all* I pray for. There are some rewards to being terribly ill, and cancer's gift to me was that it knocked me on my posterior; I landed on this sweet, old earth; and it smelled and felt wonderful. Now all I want to be is the best I can possibly be, right here, right now. Perhaps that's the quintessence of good health. When you live well and pray well, you create your own heaven, here on terra firma. And when you carry your heaven within you, as you must, eternity loses all its bluster. Perhaps we're not supposed to be able to imagine heaven, or contemplate our immortal natures. Perhaps the great beyond is meant to be a big surprise. The second great adventure.

AFTER THE BATH, EDGAR DEGAS

PERMISSIONS AND ACKNOWLEDGEMENTS

Grateful acknowledgement is made to Art Resource and Scala/Art Resource, Giraudon/ Art Resource, Herscovici/Art Resource, Erich Lessing/Art Resource and Superstock.

Grateful acknowledgement is made to Mr. Robert Bly for permission to reprint a portion of *Times Alone: Selected Poems of Antonio Machado* translated by Robert Bly, Wesleyan University Press, 1983, © 1983 by Robert Bly. All rights for the World, U.S. and Canada administered by Robert Bly. All rights reserved.